THEY MET JESUS

STUDIES IN THIS SERIES *Available from your Christian bookstore:*

they met Jesus

8 DISCUSSION STUDIES OF NEW TESTAMENT CHARACTERS

MARILYN KUNZ &
CATHERINE SCHELL

TYNDALE HOUSE
PUBLISHERS, INC.
WHEATON, ILLINOIS

Fourteenth printing, November 1981
ISBN 0-8423-7080-3
Copyright © 1968 by Marilyn Kunz and Catherine Schell
All rights reserved
Printed in the United States of America

contents

How to Use

This Discussion Guide

1/ *For groups using a rotating leadership* — Each person *must* read these pages *before* leading a study from this guide.

2/ *The purpose of this study guide* — To help the discussion leader guide others to discover for themselves what an encounter with Jesus as recorded in the Gospels may reveal about Jesus and about those who met him.

3/ *Discussion questions* — This guide provides the discussion leader with questions for the three basic areas of investigation — facts, meaning, and application. There are more questions than the leader will need, so he must *select* the questions which will help his group to cover the main point of each paragraph. Focus attention on the passage of the Bible, *not* on the study guide. An alert group will answer many of the suggested questions before they are asked. *Avoid* going woodenly through each and every question.

If everyone in the group has his own copy of the guide and has used it in study preparation for the discussion, it will be possible to discuss the contents and meaning of the passage in greater depth within the time available to the group.

The leader should never answer his own questions. He must be alert to avoid becoming a lecturer instead of a discussion leader. However, after others have made their contributions in answer to a question, the leader may add his own findings and/or restate some of the important points made by others. Sometimes a group needs *more time* than the leader realizes in order to find the answer to the questions. Sometimes the group needs a secondary or *supplementary question* such as the study guide amply provides in order to get to the heart of the paragraph.

4/ *The summary questions* — These endeavor to give *perspective* to the study of the whole lesson. Do not neglect or rush over the summary questions.

5/ *Conclusions* — The leader may use some of the ideas in the conclusion in his final remarks at the end of the study, or he may share some concluding thoughts of his own.

6/ *Reading the selections aloud* — The passages from the Bible should be read aloud by paragraphs at the start of the group study. Though people will have studied the material during the week they will need to refresh their memory in order to enter fully into the discussion. Be sure to have the reading done by paragraphs or thought units, *never* verse by verse. It is not necessary for everyone to read aloud, or for each to read an equal amount.

The reading may be done in one of two ways: read aloud all the passages for the day before discussing the questions paragraph by paragraph, or read one section aloud and discuss that portion before reading the next portion. This latter method is helpful in those lessons which include several sections from different parts of the Bible, or where two or more characters are studied.

7/ *Use of contemporary translations of the Bible* — It is strongly recommended that everyone have at least one recent translation of the Bible in addition to the King James Version or Douay Version. The questions in this study guide assume the availability of a contemporary translation.

How to Encourage Everyone to Participate

1/ Encourage discussion by asking several people to contribute answers to a question. "What do the rest of you think?" or "Is there anything else which could be added?" are ways of encouraging discussion.

2/ Be flexible and skip any questions which do not fit into the discussion as it progresses.

3/ Deal with irrelevant issues by suggesting that the purpose of your study is to discover what is *in the passage*. Suggest an informal chat about tangential or controversial issues after the regular study is dismissed.

4/ Receive all contributions warmly. Never bluntly reject

what anyone says, even if you think the answer is incorrect. Instead ask in a friendly manner, "Where did you find that?" or "Is that actually what it says?" or "What do some of the rest of you think?" Allow the group to handle problems together.

5/ Be sure you don't talk too much as the leader. Redirect those questions which are asked you. A discussion should move in the form of an asterisk, back and forth between members, not in the form of a fan, with the discussion always coming back to the leader. The leader is to act as moderator. As members of a group get to know each other better, the discussion will move more freely, progressing from the fan to the asterisk pattern.

6/ Don't be afraid of pauses or long silences. People need time to think about the questions and the passage. Never, *never* answer your own question — either use an alternate question or move on to another area for discussion.

7/ Watch hesitant members for an indication by facial expression or bodily posture that they have something to say, and then give them an encouraging nod or speak their names.

8/ Discourage too talkative members from monopolizing the discussion by specifically directing questions to others. If necessary speak privately to the over-talkative one about the need for discussion rather than lecture in the group, and enlist his aid in encouraging all to participate.

Discussion Bible Study - Advantages and Methods

What are the advantages of discussion study?

1/ People studying the Bible for the first time are often more willing to attend a discussion study than to submit to the authority of a teacher.

2/ A discussion Bible study gives opportunity for each participant to voice his questions and problems as he reacts to the passage under consideration.

3/ The degree of participation is much higher in a discussion than in a lecture form of study. Consequently there tends to be greater learning on the part of each discussion member.

What is the function of this study guide?

1/ The study guide helps a group to make new discoveries together. It directs the group into the main points of the chapter, and prevents aimless wandering and consequent wasting of time.

2/ The study guide makes it possible for each member of the group to take his turn in leading the discussion. The leader does not have to be able to lecture to the group or to explain the meaning of everything in the chapter. Rather he guides the group through the Bible passage by asking the questions from the study guide. Rotation of leadership from week to week results in greater participation and learning for each person in the group.

A group in which the discussion leadership is equally shared can continue even after the person who first initiated the group moves to another area.

What rules make for an effective discussion?

1/ Everyone in the group should *read the Bible passage* and, if possible, use the study guide in thoughtful *study* of the passage *before* coming to the group meeting.

2/ *Stick to the Bible passage under discussion.* Discover all that you can from the sections used in this study without moving around to other portions of the Bible in cross-references. This means that the person new to the Bible will not be needlessly confused, and you will avoid the danger of taking portions out of context.

3/ As your group proceeds through these studies, you will *build a common frame of reference.* Within a few weeks it will be possible for people to refer back to what they have studied together and to trace lines of thought through their common field of knowledge.

4/ *Avoid tangents.* Many different ideas will be brought to mind as you study each lesson. If an idea is not dealt with in any detail in a particular lesson, do not let it occupy long discussion that week.

5/ Since the three-fold purpose of an inductive Bible study is to discover what the Bible portion says, what it means, and what it means to you, your group should remember that *the Bible is the authority for your study.* The aim of your group should be to discover what the Bible is saying.

If you don't like something that the passage says, be honest enough to admit that you don't like it. Do not re-write the Bible to make it agree with your ideas. You may say that you do not agree with the Gospel writer or that you wish he had not said this, but don't try to make him say what he does not say. It is the Gospel accounts that you are investigating. Let them state their own case.

6/ *Apply to your own life what you discover in the study of these people who met Jesus.* Much of the vitality of any group Bible discussion depends upon honest sharing on the part of different members of the group. Discoveries made in Bible study should become guides for right action in present day life situations.

Jesus is presented ever more clearly as you move through

these eight studies, so that you have the opportunity to see the evidence that Jesus is the Messiah, the Son of God. You have the opportunity to face the implications for your life of Jesus' claims.

7/ *Let honesty with love be the attitude of your group toward one another.* Those who do not believe that Jesus is the Christ should be able to voice their doubts and questions without feeling rejected or feeling that they should cover up their true feelings. Those who do believe and are committed to Jesus as Lord and Savior should be free to share how this belief affects their lives (as appropriate to the Bible section under discussion). Rather than trying to convince one another of your beliefs or disbeliefs, you should let yourself be searched and judged by the Gospel records. You yourself should respond to Jesus as he stands revealed in these encounters with men and women of the first century.

Introduction

Honest confrontation with another person helps us in the process of self-discovery. The studies in this series are based on this principle; we in the twentieth century join men and women in the first century in dynamic experiences of encounter.

The episodes selected for study cover a wide range of situations and a remarkable variety of personalities in encounter experiences with Jesus. Men and women from strikingly different backgrounds are included. There are those of high social, economic, or political status. There are the working men and the dispossessed. Spiritually, there are the devout, the curious and questing, the proud and assured, the confused and uncertain. As we study the narratives we shall try to share in these encounters with Jesus by discovering the response of the individuals to him and his response to them.

They Met Jesus: Simeon, Anna, John the Baptist

Throughout the history of the Jewish people there were at least a few individuals in every generation who retained the expectation that Jehovah would provide a Savior for his people. They lived with such sensitivity to the reality of God that they were able to recognize his presence. Included in this number were Simeon and Anna whom we see meeting the infant Jesus as he is brought to the temple in Jerusalem in fulfillment of the law of Moses.

Jesus makes a tremendous impact on these elderly people. They do not hear him preach or see him heal, yet seeing him gives them a sense of fulfillment. They believe that all of life's questions are answered in him, that life has meaning and purpose because he has come. Though Simeon and Anna are old, they are alert to the new and startling thing that God is about to do in their world. They are not set in their ways, immovable, and convinced that all change is bad. All their lives they have worshiped the God who is Creator and they expect him to act creatively.

John the Baptist's whole life even from before his birth is linked to Jesus. Although his personal contact with Jesus (as far as the Gospels indicate) is rather limited, John is faithful to his mission of preparing the way for Jesus' public ministry.

Simeon and Anna
Luke 2:22-38

1. Why do Mary and Joseph bring Jesus to the temple at this particular time? What do you learn about Simeon? What has he been hoping and waiting for? What promise has he been

15

given? For what are men longing today? How does this affect their lives?

2. How does Simeon happen to be in the temple at the time Mary and Joseph bring Jesus there? What connection do you observe between Simeon's desire and the guidance he receives? Does the Holy Spirit guide people today? How?

3. What seven things are revealed about Jesus in the words of Simeon (verses 29-35)? In what ways are Simeon's words later fulfilled? Familiar with the Scriptures, Simeon quotes portions of Isaiah 42:6, 7; 46:13; 49:6; 52:10.

4. What do you learn about Anna (verses 36-38)? Why, do you think, is Anna permitted to be a witness to this event in the temple? What is Anna's response to this event? With whom does she share her experience? Why? What does she believe about Jesus?

5. What groups today are devoting their full energies to influencing other people? How can the committed Christian meet his responsibility to communicate the message about Jesus Christ? Give some practical suggestions.

John the Baptist
Luke 1:5-17

6. Describe the parents of John. What is foretold in verses 14-17 about John's life and ministry? Put these verses into your own words.

7. Simeon and Anna and the parents of John the Baptist are all older people who live to see the dawning of the day of the Messiah. In contrast to many older people who fear change of any kind, these four apparently rejoice in the changes which the coming of Messiah will bring. Why?

8. What qualities, do you think, enable Simeon and Anna, Zechariah and Elizabeth to recognize and to welcome the coming of the Redeemer? What can each of us do to develop a set of values which will enable us to discern the way in which God is at work in the changes we see about us?

Luke 3:1-17

9. How does John fulfill the Old Testament prophecy of verses 4-6?

10. Describe in detail the preaching of John the Baptist. What general warnings does he give? What specific advice does John have for the members of the various segments of society in his day? What do these warnings mean? What insight do they give us into what repentance means practically in our lives?

(*Note* — Luke 3:7; John takes his figure of speech from the snakes in the Jordan wilderness which would flee to safety from spreading brush fires.)

11. How does John clarify his own position and how does he describe the Christ (verses 15-17)? What balance does John's preaching suggest between faith and works?

John 1:19-36

12. What does John know about the one for whom he has been preparing the people of Israel? What has he not known (verses 31, 33)? What does John understand his job to be? What is the sign to John which identifies Jesus as the coming one? Why does John call Jesus the *Lamb of God?* What does this title mean? How does Jesus take away the sin of the world?

Matthew 11:2-6

13. What problems assail John in prison? How does John deal with his doubts? How does Jesus answer John's questions? Compare verse 5 with Isaiah 35:4-6. How should we handle doubts which especially trouble us when we are physically low? What use can we make of the Scriptures to help us?

SUMMARY

1. What do you learn about Jesus from Simeon, Anna, and John the Baptist? What can others learn about Jesus through you?

2. Consider the degree of devotion to God exhibited by Simeon, Anna, and John the Baptist. How did this prepare them to receive the news of redemption? What did they do with the news when they learned it?

CONCLUSION

Simeon, Anna, and John the Baptist represent that unique group who stood at the end of the long line of faithful people who lived under the old covenant and looked forward to the promises of a Deliverer and a Redeemer. But these three stood also at the beginning of the line of those who would live under the new covenant in which God fulfills all his promises and the pictures set forth in the old covenant. These three stood "on tiptoe," as it were, to see this fulfillment in the Lamb of God who takes away the sin of the world. The heritage of their faith has been passed on to us. It is our privilege to recognize, as they did, who Jesus is and to commit our lives to him as Savior and Lord.

They Met Jesus: The Pharisee and the Woman; the Centurion

Simon the Pharisee illustrates how a person can have close contact with Jesus, know a great deal about him, and yet completely miss out spiritually. Simon fails to respond appropriately to Jesus in the light of who Jesus is and what his own need is. Simon tries to put Jesus on trial but it becomes obvious that it is Simon himself who is on trial. The woman who comes to Jesus has a clear understanding of herself, her sin, and her need of forgiveness and cleansing from the Lord. In contrast to the Pharisee, she responds to Jesus with love and worship.

The centurion is drawn to Jesus by circumstances beyond his control. Here is a man who has a successful career, a man who wields power, but a man who has something happening within his own household which he cannot control. In this situation the centurion comes to the Lord Jesus Christ, who has ample power to cope with the problem.

The Pharisee and the Woman
Luke 7:36-50

1. As you discuss this passage using the following questions, look for the contrasting motives and actions of Simon and the woman of the city.

2. Why would Simon the Pharisee invite Jesus to his house? What does his failure to carry out the polite amenities indicate about his estimate of Jesus? Compare this to what it costs the woman socially, emotionally, and financially to express her appreciation of Jesus. What are some of the costs today for those who would serve Jesus?

3. What is Simon's response to this woman's actions? Why

does he accuse Jesus because of her actions? How does Jesus answer Simon's unspoken criticism of him and of this woman?

4. What does Jesus try to teach Simon by this illustration? What is implied about Simon in Jesus' illustration?

5. What is the reaction of those who hear Jesus' declaration that this woman's sins are forgiven? Compare with Luke 5: 20, 21.

6. Do you think that Jesus is being rude to Simon? Why does Jesus "tell it like it is"? Though Simon as a Pharisee is a highly religious man, what does he lack?

7. What does the woman reveal about herself? What does she believe about herself and about Jesus? Why is she apparently not concerned here with other people's estimate of her? Why can she be forgiven when she has lived the wrong kind of life? Is Simon forgiven? If not, why not? How do people today deal with the issues of sin and guilt in their lives?

8. Consider Jesus' claim to forgive sins. See also Luke 5:21, 24. What response does Jesus seem to look for from both Simon and the woman? What would be your response to him?

The Centurion
Matthew 8:5-13

9. What causes the centurion to come to Jesus? As a centurion, what would be his position and responsibilities in Capernaum? How would he be regarded by the Jews in Capernaum? Such concern for the welfare of a slave in that day is quite remarkable. What does it indicate about this centurion?

10. How does Jesus respond to the centurion's request? Why doesn't the sick man come to Jesus himself? What practical application does this suggest as to our own privilege and responsibility to come to Jesus on behalf of others who are in need? Describe an instance of group or individual experience of this which has been especially meaningful to you.

11. How do you account for the centurion's surprising reply in verses 8, 9? What does this reply reveal about this centurion? What is his estimate of himself and of Jesus? What does he believe about Jesus? What contrast and what comparison is he making? Describe his faith.

12. As a member of the Roman occupation army, the

centurion is aware that the Jewish laws forbid a Jew to enter the house of a Gentile. What indicates that Jesus is not bound by these traditions? Nevertheless, the centurion shows his concern for Jesus, and does not want to put him into an uncomfortable position. In what areas should we as Christians develop the courtesy of this centurion?

13. What must Jesus' demeanor be for the centurion to recognize his authority as like his own? How does Jesus react to the centurion? What important teaching does Jesus give to his followers on this occasion? How does one get into the kingdom of heaven, according to Jesus' teaching here?

SUMMARY

1. Simon the Pharisee and the centurion were both men of importance in their day. Compare their backgrounds and motives as they encountered Jesus. One invited Jesus to his home; the other did not. Yet which one came closer to Jesus? Why?

2. Describe a comparable modern situation revealing people's reactions to the claims of Jesus Christ on their lives.

3. In these two incidents, over what does Jesus demonstrate his power and authority? The problems of sin, guilt, and sickness are with us today. What is required for us to experience Jesus' action to meet these problems?

CONCLUSION

Children take tests in school which measure their intellectual standing. We have many ways in which to measure our current economic status. We are careful to have physical checkups. But what is the measure of our spiritual condition? In this study we have a good picture of three people from completely different backgrounds and ways of life, each of whom is put to the test by his confrontation with Jesus Christ. Simon the Pharisee was a man for whom religion was the most important thing in life. He invited Jesus to his home to challenge and test the latest religious phenomenon, but it was Simon who was put to the test spiritually. In his encounter with Jesus, Simon failed to recognize Jesus or to commit himself to him. Simon put his confidence in his religion instead of in the Lord.

Unlike Simon, the woman was a social and religious outcast. Her immorality had cut her off from the "good" people, but she met the test spiritually because she had an honest view of herself and her need. She recognized Jesus as worthy of her devotion and worship, and her faith in him saved her, bringing her forgiveness and peace.

The centurion, neither religious like Simon nor immoral like the woman, was apparently a man of noble qualities, yet he too had to face Jesus Christ and put his faith in him.

They Met Jesus:
a Ruler and Zacchaeus

In these passages we see Jesus meeting two wealthy men: the first, young, serious, apparently holding his wealth through inheritance; the second, a despised tax collector whose wealth has been gained through over-taxation of the community. In countries impoverished by Rome's exorbitant taxes, men readily associated the tax collector with the hated conquerors. Understandably, the wealthy tax collector was an object of hatred in Palestinian communities under Roman occupation.

We can possess things, or things can possess us. Both Zacchaeus and the ruler are owned by their possessions and ambitions, but Zacchaeus responds to Jesus' authority and is set free from his bondage. He recognizes that loyalty, worship, indeed his total person, may be yielded fully and appropriately to the Lordship of Christ.

Jesus is an idol breaker in the lives of those who let him rule. He is the real and comes to show up the false. Unless the ruler had a change of heart and came later to follow Jesus, his is one of the most tragic stories of the New Testament. The love and worship of money and what it can achieve are still a god to which many are devoting their lives.

The Ruler
Luke 18:18-30

1. Read also the parallel accounts of this incident in Matthew 19:16-22 and Mark 10:17-22. Putting together the details given in these three accounts, describe this wealthy man's encounter with Jesus.

2. How does Jesus challenge this young man to think about

the meaning of the word *good* (verse 19)? By what standard do we tend to measure our goodness? What is Jesus' standard for goodness?

3. Of the ten commandments, which does Jesus enumerate? Which does he fail to mention? See Exodus 20:1-17. With what relationship does the former set of commands deal? the latter set?

4. In his claim to have kept the commandments that deal with his relationships to his neighbors, the young man seems to indicate a shallow understanding of what these commands require. What three things does Jesus proceed to ask him to do? What *lack* in this young man is revealed by his response to Jesus' command?

5. What, essentially, does Jesus ask of this young ruler (verses 22, 23)? Compare Luke 9:23-25.

6. What does Jesus promise this rich young man if he obeys? Since the man goes away sorrowful, what is revealed about the power of possessions in his life? As you think about this incident, what place do possessions have in your life? What are your riches — family status, money, education, job, culture, home, children? What or whom do you worship?

7. Why is it hard for those who have riches to enter the kingdom of God? What picturesque exaggeration does Jesus use to describe the degree of difficulty for a rich man to enter the kingdom of God? What hope then is there for such a man?

8. What assurance does Jesus give to Peter about the cost of being his disciple (verses 28-30)? What difference would it make in your life if you realized that God is never in debt to any man, that he always gives us more than we ever give to him?

9. *To inherit eternal life* (verse 18), *to enter the kingdom of God* (verse 24), and *to be saved* (verse 26) are synonymous. Each phrase describes the same experience from a different angle. What does each description contribute to your understanding of this experience?

Zaccheus
Luke 19:1-10

10. Describe Zaccheus as to his person and his position

in society. How is his position different from that of the ruler in chapter 18? What do the two men have in common?

(*Note* — Jewish tax collectors were collaborators with the Roman conquerors. Many became rich by charging excess taxes and keeping the overcharges themselves. Jericho lay on the east-west road from the fords of Jordan to Judea, an artery of commerce where there was much to gather in customs dues.)

11. Why would Zacchaeus want to see Jesus? See Luke 5: 27-32 for the things this man may have heard to interest him in Jesus. What dissatisfaction and longings would such a man as Zacchaeus be likely to have?

12. What difficulty does Zacchaeus have in getting to see Jesus? How does he solve his problem? Imagine his feelings when Jesus stops to talk with him.

13. Why does Jesus seem to intrude so boldly into Zacchaeus' life? Describe some people today whom the Lord seems to have pulled out of their trees. Why wouldn't Zacchaeus ever have gone to Jesus the way that the ruler and Simon the Pharisee did?

14. What reveals that Zacchaeus' heart is more open to Jesus than the ruler's? What is the reaction of the bystanders to Jesus' going to this tax collector's home? Why? What is Zacchaeus' response to this criticism? What does this reveal about him? Contrast his attitude toward his material possessions with that of the young ruler when confronted by Jesus.

(*Note* — Zacchaeus' promise of restitution goes far beyond the legal penalties imposed for robbery. See Exodus 22:1.)

15. Compare the value systems of Zacchaeus and the ruler. How can you discern the value system under which a man lives today?

16. What does Jesus say about Zacchaeus' actions? In spite of the way this man is judged by others, how does Jesus judge him? See also Galatians 3:7 for the meaning of "a son of Abraham" (verse 9).

17. Why would Jesus use the phrase *to seek and to save the lost* to describe his relationship to Zacchaeus whereas he talked to the rich young ruler in terms of *entering the kingdom of God* and *having treasure in heaven?*

18. What claim does Jesus make as to his purpose in coming

and his power (verse 10)? How can we relate this to our own need of Christ?

SUMMARY

1. What does the fact that Zacchaeus is mentioned by name, but the ruler is not, suggest as to the probable lasting results of the choice which each made in the incidents described in the Gospels?

2. Suggest practical ways in which you can express your allegiance to Jesus Christ in terms of how you use your time, energy, and money.

CONCLUSION

In the Sermon on the Mount, Jesus says, "No one can be loyal to two masters. He is bound to hate one and love the other, or support one and despise the other. You cannot serve God and the power of money at the same time" (Phillips' translation). The ruler in Luke 18 found that his love of money overpowered even his highest spiritual concern. He became a slave to the things he thought he owned, for actually they owned him. Zacchaeus, on the other hand, was a man who was seeking something more in life than all his material success had been able to offer him.

They Met Jesus:
the Blind Man

The healing episode in John 9 is more than an encounter of a blind man with Jesus; here is a confrontation between the power of God and the power of authoritarian and sterile religion. The Pharisees have become so bound by the additions to the Law of God of all the small details of traditions accumulated through the centuries that they are unable to recognize the works of God in their midst.

The blind man comes to Jesus with deep physical and social needs and discovers him to be much more than a healer. In the face of much opposition and even financial pressure he comes to see the real issues involved and grows in his personal loyalty and commitment to Jesus. He refuses to be swayed by the numbers or intensity of the influential people who oppose Jesus. For those of us who are tempted to deny Jesus in the face of such pressures from society today, this blind man offers a pattern to follow.

The Blind Man
John 9:1-41

1. For background on the atmosphere in Jerusalem, read John 7:11-14, 25-27, 31, 32, 40-46. What seems to be the chief topic of conversation in Jerusalem at this time? How would this make anything Jesus says or does there of immediate significance?

2. What is the disciples' reaction to the blind man? Why does a man blind from birth pose such an interesting problem as far as the disciples are concerned?

3. What does Jesus' answer indicate about the relationship

27

between sickness and sin? Contrast with John 5:14. What should be our attitude toward sickness? See James 5:13-16.

4. What does Jesus state about himself in verses 4 and 5? Why would he make the claim, *I am the light of the world,* in this context?

5. Why would Jesus have the man go wash in the pool, rather than healing him on the spot? What would such involvement in the actual healing do for this man? How does the exercise of faith affect the one who practices it?

6. Who is stirred by the healing of the blind man? Why are the neighbors so curious and seemingly belligerent over the man's healing (verse 14)? How does the blind man explain his healing to his neighbors? How does he identify Jesus?

7. Why would the neighbors take the healed man to the Pharisees? For possible reasons, see 7:31; 9:14, 22. How do these religious authorities handle the problem (verse 16)? What is the proper place of spiritual leaders in our lives today? What benefits, dangers, and misuses of authority are possible?

8. In verses 10 to 17, what development do you observe in this formerly blind man's estimate of Jesus? Why do the Pharisees ask the healed man to evaluate Jesus?

9. How is the man's testimony received? What course do these inquisitors take? What does the reaction of the man's parents indicate about the pressures they faced? What religious pressures do people face today?

10. How do you know that the Jews here are not involved in a sincere search for the truth? Why was the prospect of being put out of the synagogue so serious in that day? How do the man's parents get off the hook?

11. What comparable reactions may men and women have today in trying to avoid the issue of who Jesus is? When does agnosticism become a refusal to know or to commit oneself?

12. What are the Jews asking the healed man to do in verse 24? Compare with what Jesus says in John 8:42.

13. Consider the claims of Jesus to be God. "So close was His connection with God that He equated a man's attitude to Himself with the man's attitude to God. Thus, to know Him

was to know God (John 8:19; 14:7). To see Him was to see God (John 12:45; 14:9). To believe in Him was to believe in God (12:44; 14:1). To receive Him was to receive God (Mark 9:37). To hate Him was to hate God (John 15:23). And to honor Him was to honor God (John 5:23)."*

14. How does the healed man differ from his parents? What danger does he face? What has it cost men through the centuries to be faithful in their commitment to Jesus Christ? What may it cost you? How does this man answer the challenge in verse 24? How does he go on to put his tormentors on the defensive? Note how his thinking about Jesus develops from verse 25a and verses 30-33.

15. How do the Jews respond to the healed man's logic? A personal attack usually is the recourse of those who are losing an argument. What does it cost this formerly blind man to decide for Jesus?

16. Why, do you think, does Jesus seek out the healed man in verse 35? What more does Jesus do for him beyond giving him his sight? Describe ways in which God seeks out men today so that they may come to truly know him.

17. Describe this healed man's final step of commitment to Jesus. Trace the three major decisions which have led him to this point.

18. In what way is Jesus Christ's coming into the world a judgment (verse 39)? How are men judged by his presence and their response to him? How did the Pharisees fail?

SUMMARY

1. Was the healed man's worship of Jesus a step of faith? In what way? What evidence do you have concerning Jesus which would help you to make an intelligent decision about committing yourself to him?

2. Describe the factors that lead to such spiritual blindness as the Pharisees exhibited.

3. The healed man could have said to himself, "I've had trouble all my life. Now that I can see, I'm not going to make

*John R. W. Stott, Basic Christianity (Chicago: Inter-Varsity Press, 1964), p. 26. Used by permission.

trouble. I'll just conform to the pressures the majority put on me. It won't really matter what I say about Jesus. In my heart I am thankful." Have you ever rationalized like this? In what situation?

CONCLUSION

Helen Keller, who was deaf and blind, wrote a poem describing the beauty of the white lily in the garden. How could she know *white?* How could she capture the lily so sensitively? In his mercy, God seems to give the blind or those otherwise deprived, special sensitivity and insight. The blind man in John 9 could see with his old inner sensitivity and his new physical sight who Jesus really was — more than man, more than prophet, the Son of God worthy of worship. In John 9:3 Jesus said that the man was blind so that the works of God could be shown in and through him. Surely this included not only the miracle of his receiving physical sight, but also the greater miracle of spiritual sight and the commitment of his life to Jesus as Lord.

They Met Jesus:
James and John

Among Jesus' group of disciples, James and John are the exuberant young hopefuls, but these thundering radicals are also vindictive, selfish, and ambitious. Along with Peter, these two brothers comprise the inner circle of Jesus' followers whom he chooses to witness certain events from which the other disciples are excluded. It should be an encouragement to most of us that James and John had such a long way to go to become truly disciplined followers of our Lord Jesus Christ.

James and John
Mark 1:16-20

1. Where does Jesus find James and John? List everything you observe about them here. Consider their probable ages, their social status, their work. What would fishermen understand Jesus to mean by the terms in which he phrases his call to them? What must this commitment to Jesus cost them? What changes would necessarily come in their lives? What adjustments and changes does everyone face as he starts a new job? What changes can be expected for anyone who follows Jesus?

2. What possible reactions may Zebedee have when his two sons leave the family business to follow Jesus? As Christian parents, what consideration should we give to the life pattern we are setting for our children? What values do we seek to teach them as they mature? Discuss specific ways in which we can help our youngsters in terms of their life work.

Mark 3:13-19

3. Describe how Jesus forms his team. For why he retires

to the hills, see Luke 6:12, 13. What three things are these apostles appointed to do? Note the order in which these three things are listed. What will this commission and its order of priorities mean for those who want to be on Jesus' team today?

4. To which of the twelve does Jesus give "nicknames"? What does the nickname given to James and John tell you about them? Why does Jesus choose them if they are indeed impetuous, unruly, and undisciplined? According to Mark 1:17, what is Jesus' purpose in choosing apostles? Why would he dare to call such a motley crew?

Matthew 17:1-8

5. For the background of this incident, read Matthew 16: 15, 16, 21-23. What should these disciples be coming to realize about Jesus? What special privilege is given James, John, and Peter? Describe the events that take place before them on this mountain. (Moses represents the Old Testament law and Elijah the prophets.) For what they discuss with Jesus see Luke 9:30, 31.

6. What happens to the *sons of thunder* when God speaks from the cloud? What do the three disciples learn about Jesus from this whole event? What comfort is there for us in how Jesus treats his frightened disciples?

Luke 9:46-56

7. Describe the attitudes of the disciples in the incidents in this section. What concerns and divides them? How can our own concern for prestige and recognition hinder our effectiveness as Christians?

8. With verses 46-48 see Mark 9:33-37, especially verse 35. What does Jesus teach his disciples about greatness? Whom do you count as great? Why? Suggest reasons why it is so difficult for the disciples and for us to follow Jesus' teaching on greatness. By what things are we confused? On what false bases do we make judgments?

9. Describe John's reaction to this teaching. What was the man doing whom John criticizes? What was this man not doing? How does John rate himself and the twelve? In what way is Christianity exclusive, and in what way is it not? How

has competition between Christians hindered the work of God?

10. How do James and John react to the snub given to Jesus by the Samaritans? List at least four things this indicates about James and John? How does this show they haven't learned the lesson on greatness? What do you imagine Jesus may have said in his rebuke of James and John?

11. How well do you receive rebukes? From whom do you accept constructive criticism most easily? When are we obligated to rebuke our fellow Christians? Give an example.

Mark 10:32-45

12. Considering what Jesus has been talking about in verses 33, 34, what do James and John reveal about themselves in verse 35? How do you react when your children make the kind of statement James and John do in verse 35? Why?

13. What do James and John want? What is commendable about their request? What is not? In answering their request, what question does Jesus ask James and John? What does their answer show about them? What apparently do they not grasp? See again verses 33, 34.

14. When Jesus says "no" to their request to sit on his right and left hand in his glory, what reasons does he give (verses 38a, 40)? What warning is there in his words? How do James and John's fellow disciples react when they hear about this request? What does this show about the other disciples?

15. Picture the scene in verses 42-45. What, do you imagine, are Jesus' emotions? the emotions of James and John? the emotions experienced by the other disciples at this point? What does Jesus want his followers to realize? What would happen in your office (factory, school) if those in positions of leadership followed the pattern which Jesus teaches? What ambitions are valid for the Christian?

16. From Mark 10:45, what is the purpose of Jesus' life and his death? How does Jesus illustrate in practice the principle he wants his followers to learn? Why do Jesus' followers always find this a difficult lesson to put into practice?

SUMMARY

1. What do you learn about the Lord Jesus Christ from

these passages which highlight his experiences with James and John? If you had only the information of these passages, what would you know about who Jesus is, what he taught, why he lived and died?

2. What kind of disciples did James and John make?

CONCLUSION

In Acts 12:2 we learn that James was the first of the twelve apostles to be martyred. He was put to death by the sword at the order of Herod. This thunderous apostle remained faithful to his Lord to his death, and did indeed drink the cup about which Jesus had warned him. John, on the other hand, lived a long life serving the Lord. The mellowing of his personality under the influence of Jesus is seen by the glimpses we catch of him leaning on Jesus' bosom at the last supper, taking responsibility for Mary from the time of the crucifixion, and the strong emphasis on love in the Gospel and letters of John.

They Met Jesus: Peter

Peter is a participant in life, not a viewer of the action. He is overtly involved with all and by all who come his way. In today's vernacular he probably would consider himself an idea man (he is a natural leader) and impetuously would offer himself to the nearest "think tank." He must often find the discipline of submitting to the authority of Jesus difficult, yet he chooses Jesus as his captain. As a disciple he may often say "But, but," though eventually he always says "Yes, Lord," never "No." Once when Jesus gives his disciples the option of leaving him, Peter says, "To whom shall we go?" Peter understands that Jesus not only is his captain but the one who alone has the words of eternal life.

Peter
Matthew 14:22-33

1. What reasons may Jesus have for sending his disciples away at this point? What would be the mood of the crowd after Jesus has fed the 5,000 (verses 15-21)? Compare with John 6:14, 15. Why would Jesus want to be alone at this time?

2. What difficulty do the disciples in the boat encounter? Why don't Jesus' followers have "storm-free" lives, even when they obey him? What comfort is there for us in the fact that when the disciples were in trouble, Jesus went to them?

3. Why should people today find it strange or impossible that the Son of God walked on water when in our time men have walked in space?

4. How do the disciples react to Jesus' walking on the sea? Describe Peter in this situation. What reasons could Peter

have for wanting to join Jesus on the water? What characteristics in Peter does this incident reveal? What series of emotions does he experience?

5. At what point does Peter begin to sink? Why doesn't he drown? What does Jesus say about Peter's experience? For what is Peter criticized? For what is he not criticized? What do the others in the boat conclude?

Luke 9:18-26

6. What two questions does Jesus put to Peter and the others (verses 18-20)? How do these two questions differ? Which one demands a personal commitment? How does Peter answer?

7. What does Jesus teach his disciples after Peter acknowledges him to be God's Messiah? What does Jesus predict will happen to him as Messiah?

8. What does Jesus teach Peter and all of us about discipleship in verses 23-26? What does it cost to be a Christian (Jesus' disciple)? What does it cost *not* to be a Christian? Why would anyone be ashamed of Jesus or of his words?

Matthew 26:30-35

9. On the night of his betrayal, for what does Jesus try to prepare the disciples (verses 31, 32)? How does Peter react to Jesus' statement? What is Peter's estimate of himself and of his fellow disciples? What is the intention of Peter's heart as revealed in his promises in verses 33, 35? What does Jesus know about Peter which Peter doesn't know about himself?

10. Note that the other disciples also claim what Peter does. What can we as Christians do about the promises we make to the Lord but fail to keep? Do you think that the Lord is surprised when we fail? Why are we so surprised? What must be the source of our power if we would stand for Christ, no matter what comes? Romans 8:35-37; Philippians 4:12, 13; Colossians 1:11, 12.

Matthew 26:56b-58, 69-75

11. Where are the other disciples when Peter follows Jesus and his captors at a distance? What does this show about

Peter? about the others?

12. Trace Peter's experience in verses 69-74. What progression do you see in his denials? Why can't Peter escape being associated with Jesus? Discuss what kind of "accent" Christians today should have which would perhaps even against their wills link them with Jesus in the minds of others.

13. What does the crowing of the cock mean to Peter? How does he react? Consider the pressures upon Christians in the twentieth century to deny Jesus in words or in deeds. How can we live so that we do not deny him?

John 21:1-25

14. What is the experience of Peter and his six friends back in Galilee? What makes Peter realize that it is Jesus waiting on the shore? How do you account for Peter's behavior in verses 7, 8?

15. Describe the scene that greets the disciples when they get to shore. How does Peter respond to what Jesus tells them to do? If we are not as eager as Peter is here to obey Jesus, can it be that we are not aware of our denials and of Jesus' forgiveness as was Peter?

16. Why would Jesus wait until breakfast is finished before he has his conversation with Peter? Why would Jesus address Peter as *Simon, son of John*? What must Peter consider if *these* to which Jesus refers (verse 15) are the boat, the nets, fish, and Peter's fishing career to which he has momentarily returned? What does Peter have to think about if *these* means his fellow disciples?

17. When Jesus for the third time questions Peter's love, how does Peter respond? What change do you observe in Peter here from the time described in Matthew 26:33, 35?

18. Why would Jesus ask Peter the same question three times? What has Peter recently done three times to Jesus? What assignment does Jesus give to Peter in recommissioning him as an apostle? See 1 Peter 5:1-4 for how Peter's advice years later to fellow Christians is influenced by this experience with Christ.

19. Although Peter is now much less sure of himself than he was before the crucifixion, the Lord predicts that Peter will

be a faithful servant to his death. What is Jesus' answer to Peter's question about the future of his fellow disciple? What is Jesus' advice to each Christian who focuses his attention on his fellow Christians rather than upon the Lord?

SUMMARY

1. What would you say was Peter's greatest strength, and his greatest weakness? Why is a man's weakness often the corruption of his area of greatest strength? Describe Peter's experience of the grace of God.

2. From the incidents in Peter's life considered in this study, what is revealed about Jesus Christ? What will it mean in your life if you acknowledge Jesus as the Son of God as Peter did?

CONCLUSION

"How do I know that God is good? I don't.
I gamble like a man. I bet my life
Upon one side in life's great war. I must,
I can't stand out. I must take sides. The man
Who is a neutral in this fight is not
A man. He's bulk and body without breath,
Cold leg of lamb without mint sauce. A fool.
He makes me sick. Good Lord! Weak tea!
     Cold slops!
I want to live, live out, not wobble through
My life somehow, and then into the dark.
I must have God. . . .
Well — God's my leader, and I hold that He
Is good, and strong enough to work His plan
And purpose out to its appointed end.
I am no fool, I have my reasons for
This faith, but they are not the reasonings,
The coldly calculated formulae
Of thought divorced from feeling. They are true,
Too true for that. . . .
I can't stand shiv'ring on the bank, I plunge
Head first. I bet my life on Beauty, Truth,
And Love, not abstract but incarnate Truth,

Not Beauty's passing shadow but its Self.
Its very self made flesh, Love realised.
I bet my life on Christ — Christ crucified."

These words by G. A. Studdert Kennedy, chaplain in World War I, in his poem, "Faith," could be Peter's testimony in twentieth century language.

They Met Jesus: Pilate

Pilate is a man who has learned to live by his wits in the complicated political situation of his day. He is smart and a calculator. He isn't one to "blow his cool," but he finds Jesus disturbing — a king, but not the sort of king with whom Pilate is accustomed to dealing! Pilate is after all a *practical* man in the worst sense of the word. Truth to him is a secondary issue overshadowed by expediency. He is so involved in the pattern of life from which Jesus would call him that he cannot or will not respond to Jesus' personal challenge to him. Pilate would be astonished to know that his place in history will depend solely on the fact that he has something to do with Jesus who is called the Christ.

Pilate
John 18:28—19:16

(For background information, you will find it helpful to read Mark 15:1-15 and Luke 23:1-25 in preparation for this study.)

1. Who are *they* in verse 28, and where do they take Jesus? Why? See 18:12, 13, 24. The Praetorium was the residence of the Roman provincial governor, Pilate, who stayed in Jerusalem to keep order during the Passover season when national feeling ran high. Why don't the members of the Jewish council enter Pilate's house?

2. Where does the interview with Pilate take place? What irony is there in this situation? Name some flagrant inconsistencies in religious people today. How can we make sure we aren't guilty of such inconsistencies?

3. What do you learn from the first exchange between Pilate and the Jewish leaders? What can you surmise about

41

their relationship with Pilate from this conversation? *Note* — "The procurator (Pilate) had full powers of life and death, and could reverse capital sentences passed by the Sanhedrin, which had to be submitted to him for ratification" (New Bible Commentary).

Compare verse 32 with John 3:14 and 12:32, 33. What does Jesus know that neither Pilate nor the Jews know at this point?

4. Where does the interview between Pilate and Jesus take place? Where are the Jews? What is Pilate's question to Jesus? Compare with the question asked of Jesus by the High Priest in Mark 14:61. Why is Pilate concerned about *king* rather than *Christ* or *Messiah*? What is Pilate's business?

5. What does Jesus mean by his question in verse 34? What opportunity is Jesus giving to Pilate? How does Pilate answer? If you were directing a film of this scene, what mood would you try to get Pilate to convey at this moment?

6. What does Jesus tell Pilate about his kingship? What does Jesus want Pilate to realize? What position of power does Jesus suggest he has?

7. What confidence does Jesus have in his followers (verse 36)? As Christians how can we know what course of action our King would have us to take in times of danger to ourselves and our property? Consider several specific situations such as housing, school busing, crime, Viet Nam, etc.

8. What does Pilate's response in verse 37 indicate? Instead of repeating his defense that his kingdom is not of this world, Jesus seeks to confront Pilate with spiritual realities. What does Jesus tell Pilate? For "the truth" of which Jesus speaks, see John 3:31-36.

9. Suggest at least two different ways in which one might read Pilate's words in verse 38. What would each way of reading suggest about Pilate and his spiritual state?

10. What is Pilate's conclusion concerning Jesus (verse 38)? What should Pilate's next step be in the light of his authority and of Roman justice? Instead, how does Pilate seek to avoid taking a clear stand (verse 39)? Why? Discuss the weakness of Pilate at this point. What qualities are necessary in a person if he would exert right leadership under pressure?

11. What results from Pilate's attempt to placate the Jews? See also Mark 15:6-15.

John 19:1-22, 31-33, 38

12. Describe the scene in verses 4-6. How do you account for Pilate's having Jesus scourged? What is Pilate's intention (Luke 23:16)? What judicial statement does Pilate make three times? (John 18:38b; 19:4, 6) In the light of this, what should Pilate do? Why does he fail? What emotion begins to dominate Pilate? Why? (See also Matthew 27:19.)

13. What causes Pilate to ask Jesus where he is from? How does Pilate react when Jesus does not answer? Why?

14. How is Pilate affected by Jesus' answer to his threat? Who is the prisoner in this situation? Why?

15. What ultimate threat do the Jews use against Pilate? Why is their apparent concern for Caesar's position flagrant hypocrisy? Why does Pilate succumb? See also Matthew 27:24a.

16. Why is the drop-out phenomenon which Pilate exhibits still prevalent in society? How can a responsible Christian help those who are tempted to abdicate responsibility, whether businessmen or housewives or young people?

17. What last attempt to set Jesus free does Pilate make in verses 13-15? Why does this fail? To whom does Pilate abdicate his authority? Why? See also Matthew 27:24, 25. What difficulties will Pilate doubtless have when he tries to exert his authority in Jerusalem in future situations? Why?

SUMMARY

1. What people do you know today who have the same traits and problems which Pilate had? What spiritual opportunities did Pilate have? What specifically did Pilate know about Jesus from the reports of the Jews, from Jesus himself, and from his own observations of Jesus and those who opposed Jesus? What decision did Pilate make about Jesus? What decision did he fail to make? Describe someone today who may be in a similar position in his relationship to Jesus.

2. Today we hear much about law and justice. How would

you illustrate a talk on this subject from the passages studied in this lesson?

CONCLUSION

Amazingly, Pilate receives much gentler treatment from the followers of Jesus than from secular historians. In addition to pointing out instances of Pilate's ineptness as a governor and his stupidity in dealing with the Jews, the Jewish historian Philo describes Pilate "by nature rigid and stubbornly harsh" and "of spiteful disposition and an exceeding wrathful man" and speaks of "the bribes, the acts of pride, the acts of violence, the outrages, the cases of spiteful treatment, the constant murders without trial, the ceaseless and most grievous brutality of which the Jews might accuse him."

This surely tells us something of the restraint with which the New Testament writers wrote. But even more significant, the record of Pilate's interviews with Jesus tells us about the demeanor and person of our Lord Jesus Christ as we see him reflected in the eyes of a man like Pilate. Even a man like the one Philo describes was transformed, softened, made uneasy, challenged by the presence of the Lord Jesus. How great was Pilate's loss that he did not submit himself to Jesus Christ rather than to the political pressures about him!

They Met Jesus:
Philip and Thomas

Discipleship is difficult for Philip and Thomas. It must seem to them that Jesus often demands the unreasonable. Not content to leave them with the degree of commitment and faith they already have, Jesus constantly stretches their faith. Philip and Thomas are realists and practical men, men who face facts, who are not given to sentimentality, so Jesus meets them with facts, with the practical expression of his power. When Thomas becomes convinced of the resurrection and acknowledges Jesus as Lord and God, he leads the way for thousands of skeptics, many like C. S. Lewis, who said of himself that he came kicking and screaming into the kingdom of God.

Philip
John 1:43-51

1. Describe Philip's call to be a disciple. What is his first act as a disciple? What does he apparently understand about what it means to follow Jesus? What does Philip tell Nathanael about Jesus? Why is Nathanael skeptical?

2. What is Philip's answer to Nathanael's skepticism? What confidence does Philip have? How can we emulate Philip as we attempt to tell others about Jesus?

3. What, do you imagine, are Philip's reactions to the meeting between Jesus and Nathanael? What does Nathanael recognize about Jesus? Why? Consider the temptation to Philip to interfere in this conversation. Who convinces Nathanael? How can we know when to keep quiet, and how can we bring people to the place where Jesus can convince them of who he is?

John 6:1-14

4. Why are the multitudes following Jesus at this point in his ministry? What indicates the crowd's eagerness to find him?

What is Jesus' reaction to the crowd?

5. What question does Jesus ask Philip? Of what sort of man would you ask such a question? What information or abilities does Philip perhaps have? In what way, do you think, does Jesus want to test Philip? How does Philip answer? What does his answer show? Contrast the significance of Philip's answer and Andrew's suggestion.

6. Consider the use Jesus makes of Andrew's discovery of the boy with a lunch. Why is Philip unable to contribute positively to the situation? What opportunity does he miss? Why? Discuss how we can better meet the tests the Lord gives us through the circumstances of need in our own lives and the lives of others.

John 12:20-26

7. What may it indicate about Philip that of all the disciples, the Greeks choose to approach him to request an interview with Jesus? What suggests that Philip feels unsure as to how to handle their request? What do you do when you are unsure about the Lord's will in a particular situation? What do Philip and Andrew do?

8. What does it mean to Jesus that these representatives of the Gentile world want to see him? What does Jesus teach here about himself? What does he teach about those who serve him? What does Jesus promise?

John 14:6-11

9. Consider the claim of Jesus in verse 6. How does this answer the often-heard statement that there are many ways to God? What does verse 7 add to Jesus' claim in verse 6?

10. What do you think that Philip has in mind by his implied request in verse 8? How does Jesus answer Philip? What has Philip failed to *see?* What evidence has been given to Philip? What two reasons for belief does Jesus suggest to him in verse 11?

Thomas
John 11:5-8, 14-16

11. Why are the disciples afraid for Jesus to go to Judea again? How does Thomas react when he sees Jesus is deter-

mined to go to Bethany in spite of the fact that Lazarus is dead? What loyalty does Thomas put before his personal safety? What does he think is going to happen? What other characteristic of Thomas besides loyalty is seen here?

12. Through the years Christians have been accused variously of being "Pollyannas," or of being fatalists. How would you describe the Christian philosophy of life?

John 20:19-31

13. Describe Jesus' resurrection appearance to the disciples in verses 19-23. How is their mood changed by the appearance of the Lord? What commission does he give them and how does he empower them for the job?

14. Imagine several possible reasons why Thomas is not present with the disciples when Jesus appears to them. Remember the mood of the disciples as suggested by verse 19.

15. If you were writing a script for the scene outlined in verses 24, 25, how would you develop the argument and the emotional conflict between Thomas and the others? Describe Thomas' position. In what way is he rejecting his fellow disciples by his position? How has Thomas' earlier pessimism about the danger to Jesus in Judea proved correct? Why doesn't Thomas just say that he believes in order to please the others?

16. What would Thomas' week between verse 25 and verse 26 be like? What do we owe Thomas for his uncompromising honesty? How do you know Thomas doesn't completely withdraw from the society of his fellow-Christians in spite of the discomfort he must feel in their presence?

17. What does the risen Lord know about his servant Thomas? Why does he use Thomas' own words in verse 27? What does Thomas do? When and how is he convinced? Consider Thomas' words as he, a Jew, acknowledges the risen Jesus to be God.

18. What comment does Jesus make on Thomas' faith? According to verses 30, 31, why was the Gospel of John written? What opportunity and what promise are ours?

SUMMARY

1. What similarities do you notice between Philip and Thomas? Describe some people today who are like them in

their approach to Christianity. How did Jesus handle their practical "it can't be done, you've got to prove it to me" attitudes? What did Philip and Thomas learn about Jesus? Be specific from the incidents discussed.

2. If you are a hardheaded realist like Philip and Thomas, consider these points made by John Stott in his booklet, *Becoming a Christian*. "The Lord Jesus Himself constantly discouraged people from following Him if they were in danger of being swept into His allegiance by irresponsible emotion. . . . What demands does Christ make on me, both at the time of accepting Him, and afterwards? (1) I must repent of my sin. "Repent and believe," he said (Mark 1:15). The faith which receives Christ must be accompanied by the repentance which rejects sin. . . . (2) I must surrender to Christ. He wants to be my Lord as well as my Saviour. . . . (3) I must confess Christ before men. I realize that I cannot be a secret disciple."**

CONCLUSION

At the feeding of the five thousand, Philip evaluated the situation in terms of dollars and cents. He could see only that it would take six months' wages to feed the crowd. He lacked the spiritual insight to see the possibilities for the power of Jesus in a boy's lunch. How often we are hindered by a calculation of the facts which leaves out the fact of God. Although through the years Thomas has had to bear the adjective "doubting" in the situation described in John 20, he showed virtues we can well emulate. Thomas showed balance and maturity in not being swept up in the enthusiasm of the other disciples because he first wanted to test the truth. Yet he did not withdraw himself from the influence of the Christian fellowship with whom he was temporarily in conflict. Once convinced of the truth that Jesus was alive from the dead, Thomas committed himself wholly, acknowledging Jesus as his Lord and God.

**John R. W. Stott, *Becoming a Christian* (Chicago: Inter-Varsity Press, 1950), pp. 11-13. Used by permission.